Do You KNOW?™

NEW YORK CITY

A challenging little quiz on the hustle and bustle, glitz and glamour, faces and places of our #1 city

SOURCEBOOKS, INC.®
NAPERVILLE, ILLINOIS

Published by Sourcebooks, Inc.
P.O. Box 4410, Naperville, Illinois 60567-4410
(630) 961-3900
Fax: (630) 961-2168
www.sourcebooks.com

Printed and bound in the United States of America
SP 10 9 8 7 6 5 4 3 2 1

If you live in a place for a while, or visit often, you might be surprised how much you pick up about its people, places, and things, about its local history and expressions, movies and songs, politicians and music makers, churches and comedy clubs, stadiums and suburbs, slogans and snacks—the many parts of the whole. Of course, you might also be surprised at what you *haven't* learned.

In this New York City quiz you'll find questions in both categories. Some are easy. Some will give even a native trouble. Of course, one person's "That's simple!" can be another's "Huh?" The questions are all over the lot, so it's fun to try them alone or with others.

One thing that's pretty certain: Everyone who submits to the test—home-grown, transplant, or frequent visitor—will meet some stumpers. Even if you breeze through the first few questions you look at, get ready for some head scratching. And maybe you'll learn a thing or two.

So here are 100 questions. Count ten points for each correct answer. Where a question has more than one part, you'll be told how to divide the credit. Here and there you'll find a chance to earn five or ten bonus points, so it's theoretically possible to score more than 1,000. (But you won't!)

Figure your performance this way:

Above 900:	**Spectacular!**
700–899:	A very solid showing.
500–699:	Nothing to be ashamed of.
Below 500:	Told you it was tough.

1. What colors are Sabrett pushcart umbrellas?

a. Red, white, and blue

b. Red and white

c. White and blue

d. Yellow and blue

2. Last name of radio DJ "Cousin Brucie":

a. Williams

b. Freed

c. Morrow

d. Gossert

3. Do you talk New York? For two points each:

a. What's a sandwich on a long roll? _____

b. What do you call the front steps? _____

c. At the bank or at a movie theater, you wait _____ line.

d. If you don't want to walk, catch the bus, or take a taxi, you'll take the

_____

e. You've answered these all correctly? Well good _____ you!

4. On airline schedules and tickets, New York's biggest airport is written as "JFK." But do you know the three-letter codes for the other major airports in the area? Five points apiece.

LaGuardia: _____

Newark: _____

5. What color is a Spaldeen?

_____

6. On which TV channel *hasn't* Ernie Anastos read the news?

a. 2 (WCBS)

b. 4 (WNBC)

c. 5 (WNYW)

d. 7 (WABC)

e. 9 (WWOR)

7. For five points apiece, where's Duffy Square and why is there always a line there? (Ten bonus points if you know Duffy's occupation.)

_____

_____

8. Where did hip-hop begin? (For five bonus points each, which neighborhoods claim Jay-Z, 50 Cent, and Run-D.M.C.?)

    a. Bed-Stuy, Brooklyn
    b. The South Bronx
    c. West Harlem
    d. Hollis, Queens
    e. South Jamaica, Queens

9. For two points apiece, match the murder victim and the place of his demise:

a. Joey Gallo	f. Park Sheraton Hotel barbershop
b. Albert Anastasia	g The Dakota
c. Paul Castellano	h. Umberto's Clam House
d. John Lennon	i. Spark's Steak House
e. Malcolm X	j. Audubon Ballroom

10. The city's police are "New York's Finest"; firefighters are "New York's Bravest"; sanitation workers are "New York's Strongest." What, then, are prison guards in the Department of Correction?

_____

11. Fill in the same word on each line and you'll have the name of *two* places where you can get a hot dog and a juice drink.

    a. Gray's _____

    b. _____ King

12. Five bits of New York that are sometimes known by their initials. You get two points for each correct ID.

    a. GWB (a river crossing): _____

    b. CPW (a residential street): _____

    c. BAM (a performing arts hall): _____

    d. MOMA (a cultural repository): _____

    e. SNL (a weekly show): _____

13. Speaking of initials, in New York TLC does not mean tender loving care. It means:

_____

14. In which boroughs did these old-time TV sitcoms take place?

    a. *All in the Family*: _____

    b. *The Honeymooners*: _____

    c. *The Odd Couple*: _____

    d. *Welcome Back, Kotter*: _____

    e. *Car 54, Where Are You?*: _____

15. And in the world of comics, what's Spider-Man's home borough? (Five bonus points if you know the neighborhood.)

_____

16. For five points each, which New York newspaper:

    a. Published an editorial congratulating the Red Sox for beating the Yankees in the '03 American League pennant race… after the *Yanks* won:

    _____

    b. Memorably headlined, during the city's fiscal crisis in the '70s, *"FORD TO CITY: DROP DEAD"*:

    _____

    (For five extra points, what paper ran this headline over its version of the same story: *"Ford, Castigating City, Asserts He'd Veto Fund Guarantee; Offers Bankruptcy Bill"?*)

17. When and why do teams inflate huge balloons around the American Museum of Natural History?

_____

18. What New York thoroughfare is nicknamed "The Boulevard of Death" because of a history of pedestrian fatalities?

_____

19. Finish the come-on of dermatologist Jonathan Zizmor ("Dr. Z"), as seen in subways and on the telly for decades: "Now you can have _____ _____!"

20. For two points each, place the "Hill" neighborhoods in their boroughs:

    a. Lighthouse Hill   f. Bronx
    b. Sugar Hill   g. Brooklyn
    c. Castle Hill   h. Manhattan
    d. Ocean Hill   i. Queens
    e. Richmond Hill   j. Staten Island

21. **Five places and institutions with New York streets in their names. For two points each, match them.**

    a. 92nd Street
    b. 79th Street
    c. 145th Street
    d. Second Avenue
    e. Bank Street

    f. Bridge
    g. College of Education
    h. Y
    i. Deli
    j. Boat Basin

22. **Pick the one name on the list that *hasn't* been used for a New York pizzeria:**

    a. Ray's Pizza
    b. Famous Ray's Pizza
    c. Ray's Famous Pizza
    d. Famous Original Ray's Pizza
    e. Most Famous Ray's Pizza
    f. Original Ray's Pizza

    g. New York Ray's Pizza
    h. Harlem's Ray's Pizza
    i. World Famous Ray's Pizza
    j. Best Ray's Pizza
    k. Ray's Real Pizza
    l. Ray Bari Pizza

23. **For five points each, who said it?**

    a. "How'm I doin'?" _____

    b. "Only the little people pay taxes." _____

24. **Where might you be "just kickin' down the cobblestones, lookin' for fun and feelin' groovy"?**

    _____

25. Five quick questions about The Dakota, one of Manhattan's great old apartment houses. Two points per answer.

a. What 1968 movie with Mia Farrow includes scenes of the building's exterior? _____

b. Who was murdered in front of the building in 1980?

_____

c. The Dakota is on the _____ corner of 72nd Street and Central Park West.

d. What landscaped area across the street in Central Park memorializes a former resident of the building?

_____

e. Why is The Dakota called The Dakota?

_____

26. Could you do the job of a New York postal carrier? Choose the right street addresses, for two points each:

a. Macy's

b. The Waldorf-Astoria

c. Bloomingdale's

d. Elaine's

e. The Empire State Building

f. 1000 Third Avenue

g. 1703 Second Avenue

h. 350 Fifth Avenue

i. 301 Park Avenue

j. 151 West 34th Street

27. Everyone knows it as "Grand Central," but what's its proper name?

a. Grand Central Station

b. Grand Central Railway Station

c. Grand Central Terminal

d. Grand Central Depot

e. The Grand Central

28. What night of the week is Amateur Night at the Apollo?

_____

29. New York has the baseball Mets at Shea Stadium, of course. But there are Mets also on Fifth Avenue and at Lincoln Center. For five points each, which Mets are they?

Fifth Avenue: _____

Lincoln Center: _____

30. Five fill-ins, worth two points apiece:

a. The Cathedral of St. John the Divine is jokingly called "St. John the _____."

b. Music lovers can visit the graves of Fritz Kreisler, Irving Berlin, George M. Cohan, Miles Davis, Duke Ellington, Lionel Hampton, and W.C. Handy in the Bronx, in _____ Cemetery.

c. Old Con Ed slogan: "Dig we must, for a _____ _____ _____."

d. Unlike New England clam chowder, the Manhattan version contains no _____.

e. The Hall of Fame for Great Americans is on the grounds of _____ _____ _____.

31. The New York names on the left should bring to mind one of the words or phrases on the right. Two points for each match.

a. Barney Greengrass   f. cigars
b. Nat Sherman   g. talk radio
c. Danny Meyer   h. smoked fish
d. Caroline Hirsch   i. standup comedy
e. Joan Hamburg   j. upscale restaurants

32. How would you describe Crazy Eddie's prices: _____

33. Arrange these seven neighborhoods from farthest downtown to farthest uptown. For ten points, put them in perfect order.

   a. El Barrio
   b. Chelsea
   c. Tribeca
   d. Inwood
   e. Yorkville
   f. Murray Hill
   g. Washington Heights

34. And for two points each, explain the origins of these neighborhood names:

   a. Soho: _____

   b. Tribeca: _____

   c. Nolita: _____

   d. Dumbo: _____

   e. Alphabet City: _____

35. Which statement *isn't* true?

   a. Central Park is bigger than Monaco.
   b. The Statue of Liberty's index finger is eight feet long.
   c. Brooklyn was once the capital of the United States of America.
   d. Times Square used to be called Longacre Square.

36. Where might you see a plaque with this legend?

> THE HIGHEST
> NATURAL POINT
> ON MANHATTAN
> 265.05 FEET
> ABOVE SEA LEVEL

37. Warner Wolf's catchphrase: "Let's go to the _____!"

38. How much does it cost to ride the Staten Island Ferry?

    a. $2.50   d. $0.05
    b. $1.25   e. $0.00
    c. $0.50

39. Who, over a period of more than half a century, wore the uniforms of all four New York major league baseball teams: Dodgers, Giants, Mets, and Yankees?

    C_____ S_____

40. For five points each, what subway lines go to Shea Stadium and Aqueduct Racetrack?

    Shea: _____

    Aqueduct: _____

41. The names Lindy's, Junior's, and Reuben's should make you think of what dessert?

    _____

42. The borough of the Bronx was named for a Danish settler named Bronck. What was Bronck's first name?

    a. Charles   d. Richmond
    b. Jonas   e. No one knows
    c. Grayson

43. **Each of the words on the left goes with one of the words on the right. You get two points for each correct match:**

a. Hampton   f. Mann
b. Mitchell   g. Bay
c. Horace   h. Jitney
d. City   i. Island
e. Sheepshead   j. Lama

44. **Taking inspiration from Jackie Gleason, the borough greets visitors and returning residents with signs reading "Welcome to Brooklyn—**

_____ _____

_____ _____ !"

45. **Long-time slogan of WINS news radio: "You give us 22 minutes, we'll give you**

_____
_____."

46. **Five points for telling which stores hand out these New York icons:**

a. Robin's-egg blue bags and boxes: _____

b. Brown shopping bags labeled "BIG BROWN BAG," "MEDIUM BROWN BAG," and "LITTLE BROWN BAG": _____

47. **What special names have been given to these Manhattan locations? Two points for each correct match.**

a. W. 32nd between 5th & Broadway   f. Seminary Row
b. W. 66th between Columbus & Central Park W.   g. WC Handy's Place
c. W. 52nd at Seventh   h. Joey Ramone Place
d. E. 2nd at Bowery   i. Korea Way
e. W. 122nd between Amsterdam and Riverside   j. Peter Jennings Way

48. Who *hasn't* had a street designated in his honor? (Just one.)

    a. Louis Armstrong
    b. Antonin Dvofiák
    c. Nikola Tesla
    d. Christopher Columbus
    e. Regis Philbin
    f. Edgar Allen Poe
    g. Charles Lindbergh
    h. Isaac Bashevis Singer

49. What's the name of the foppish cartoon mascot of *The New Yorker*, who appears on the cover every year on the magazine's anniversary?

E_____ T_____

50. For which team *didn't* Marty Glickman regularly call the action or do a pre- or post-game show?

    a. Devils
    b. Dodgers
    c. Giants
    d. Jets

    e. Knicks
    f. UConn football
    g. Yankees
    h. Yonkers Raceway

51. What's the celebratory name for the stretch of lower Broadway where ticker tape parades are held?

"_____ of _____"

52. Complete the almost-rhyming couplet on the famous sign in the window of Katz's Delicatessen, first installed during World War II. (Ten-point bonus: What much-discussed scene from a movie written by Nora Ephron and directed by Rob Reiner took place at a table in Katz's?)

Send a salami

_____

53. Who wrote the poem at the base of the Statue of Liberty? ("Give me your tired, your poor, your huddled masses yearning to breathe free")

    a. Ralph Waldo Emerson   d. Walt Whitman
    b. Emily Dickinson   e. Jack Handey
    c. Emma Lazarus

54. If you're deep in Central Park, how can you tell what cross street you're near?

_____

55. What's the next number in this series: 14, 23, 28, 34, 42, 50, _____?

56. The New York AM radio dial is flooded with all manner of station formats. In the short list below, two stations are all news, two are news and talk, and two are sports. Say which is which. Two points apiece, so yes, you can rack up a dozen points here.

    a. 660: _____
    b. 710: _____
    c. 770: _____
    d. 880: _____
    e. 1010: _____
    f. 1050: _____

57. On May 19, 1962, Marilyn Monroe sang "Happy Birthday" in front of a New York crowd. Even today, a recording of that breathy rendition is occasionally played, and the performance is often parodied, imitated, and referenced. Where and to whom did M.M. sing?

_____

58. A famous movie chase scene was filmed in Brooklyn along the elevated BMT West End line. Name that flick. (Hint: Gene Hackman)

_____

59. Where is Manhattan's only lighthouse?

_____

60. What's the popular name for the Fuller Building, at 175 Fifth Ave.?

_____

61. What do apartment dwellers call a diagonal steel rod that bars entry by bracing the door against a plate in the floor?

_____

62. What do the initials in PATH stand for?

_____

63. The Gay Liberation Front was formed in New York in 1969, shortly after a violent raid on The _____ Inn on _____ Street. (Five points for each part.)

64. Two of these river crossings carry subway trains as well as individual vehicles. Five points apiece if you can pick them out of the list.

    a. Manhattan Bridge
    b. Brooklyn Bridge
    c. Williamsburg Bridge

    d. Queensboro Bridge
    e. Madison Avenue Bridge
    f. University Heights Bridge

65. Name the residence hotel that at one time or another sheltered Mark Twain, Jack Kerouac, Bob Dylan, Jane Fonda, and Sid Vicious.

    _____

66. What's the real name of the veteran TV weather guy called "Mr. G."?

    I_____ G_____

67. For two points each, match the old names (on the left) with the new (on the right):

    a. Pan Am
    b. Idlewild
    c. Central Park
    d. AT&T
    e. Hell's Kitchen

    f. John F. Kennedy
    g. Sony
    h. MetLife
    i. Clinton
    j. Jacqueline Kennedy Onassis

68. Exterior shots of "Monk's Coffee Shop" on this TV sitcom actually show the outside of Tom's Restaurant, Broadway at 112th Street. Name the sitcom. (For five bonus points, who wrote and sang a much-discussed pop song said to refer to the same Tom's?)

    _____

69. When traffic broadcasters talk about "the Willy B," what do they mean? How about "the George"? Five points each.

"The Willy B": _____

"The George": _____

70. What fictional sex columnist supposedly lives at 245 East 73rd Street in Manhattan?

_____

71. Major Deegan, who has a highway named for him, was an army major during World War I. What rank was Goethals, who can claim a New York bridge?

_____

72. In *Guys and Dolls*, where did Nathan Detroit want to hold "the oldest established permanent floating crap game in New York"? (Hint: He and his gambling pals had to relocate because they couldn't come up with the grand the owner demanded— in advance.)

_____

73. The column that appears regularly beneath the weekly restaurant review in the *New York Times* is labeled:

   a. "ANOTHER RESTAURANT TO CONSIDER"
   b. "CHEAP EATS"
   c. "MEALS FOR LESS THAN $20"
   d. "$25 AND UNDER"
   e. "GOOD VALUE"

74. What musical show ran for 42 years at the Sullivan Street Playhouse?

_____

75. Match the neighborhood to the ethnic group:

a. Arthur Avenue, Bronx   f. Russian
b. Astoria, Queens   g. Italian
c. Brighton Beach, Brooklyn   h. Chinese
d. Flushing, Queens   i. Indian
e. Jackson Heights, Queens   j. Greek

76. He became so famous for his stunt, back in the 19th century, that his name was turned into a popular expression meaning to perform a dangerous act—like jumping off a bridge into a river. Who was he?

S_____ B_____

77. What jazz standard, popularized by Duke Ellington, was named for a subway line?

_____
_____

78. Five points each for identifying these two long-ago New York sports figures by their nicknames:

"The Pearl": E_____ M_____

"Broadway Joe": J_____ N_____

79. What's at the southernmost end of Fifth Avenue? (Hint: It's named for a president.)

_____

80. Which one is commonly referred to as "The Street"?

a. 42nd Street

b. Wall Street

c. Delancey Street

d. Madison Avenue

e. Broadway

81. The flavors: black cherry, orange, root beer, ginger ale, Cel-Ray, and cream soda. The brand?

_____

82. Which park is larger, the Bronx's Van Cortlandt or Brooklyn's Prospect?

_____

83. Four blanks are New York streets, one a park. Each line is a movie title. Two points for each movie you can name.

a. *Miracle on* _____

b. *Crossing* _____

c. *Slaughter on* _____

d. _____ *Danny Rose*

e. *The Panic in* _____

84. For two points apiece, match the lyric snippet to the song title:

a. "Remember me to Herald Square"

b. "The rumble of the subway trains"

c. "We'll go to Coney and eat baloney on a roll"

d. "These vagabond shoes are longing to stray"

e. "I'm taking a Greyhound on the Hudson River line"

f. "Manhattan" (Lorenz Hart)

g. "New York State of Mind" (Billy Joel)

h. "Lullaby of Broadway" (Al Dubin)

i. "Give My Regards to Broadway" (George M. Cohan)

j. "New York, New York" (Fred Ebb)

85. For five points each, where does the New York Marathon start, and where does it finish?

Start: _____

Finish: _____

86. What venerable New York bookshop measures its books for sale in miles?

_____

87. For five points apiece, finish these slogans *and* name the businesses:

a. "An educated consumer is _____ _____ _____."

(_____)

b. _____ _____ _____, move closer to me."

(_____)

88. The metal label affixed to the hood of every yellow cab in New York City, which authorizes the driver to respond to passengers who hail from the curb, is called a:

a. license   d. fleet key
b. label   e. bonnet tag
c. medallion

89. Broadcaster, actress, and Rudy's wife #2:

D_____ H_____

90. Known for her home for unwanted kids:

M_____ H_____

91. Match the school with its celebrated alum, for two points apiece:

a. Barbra Streisand
b. Woody Allen
c. Kareem Abdul-Jabbar
d. Barry Manilow
e. Henry Winkler

f. Power Memorial
g. Erasmus Hall
h. Eastern District
i. McBurney School
j. Midwood

92. Fay Wray is to the Empire State Building as Jessica Lange is to the _____ _____ _____ as Naomi Watts

is to the _____ _____ _____.

93. Kossar's is to bialys as Manganaro's is to _____

as John's on Bleecker is to _____.

94. For five points each, name a New York private school known by a diminutive and a color, and a former New York mayor known by the same diminutive and something that grows in a garden.

School: _____ _____   Ex-mayor: _____ _____

95. Central Park and Prospect Park both have a designated spot for the activity, and under the same name, but you can't do it all year round. Explain.

_____

96. On which one of these holidays are alternate side parking rules *not* suspended in the five boroughs?

a. Ash Wednesday
b. Purim
c. Patriot Day

d. Idul-Fitr
e. Diwali

97. "I'll meet you under the clock." Explain. (Five bonus points: How many faces does that clock have?)

_____

98. Which of these *isn't* the name of a Trump property in New York City?

a. Trump Tower
b. Trump International Hotel and Tower
c. Trump Parc and Trump Parc East
d. Trump Park Avenue

e. Trump Place
f. Trump World Tower
g. Trump Universal City

99. What kind of animals, portrayed in stone, guard the main entrance of the New York Public Library on Fifth Avenue? (Ten bonus points if you know their names.)

_____

100. Which is the most common type of cockroach in New York City?

a. American
b. Asian
c. Australian
d. brown-banded

e. German
f. Madagascar hissing
g. Oriental
h. Pennsylvania woods

ANSWERS

1. d.

2. c.

3. a. a *hero*, b. the *stoop*, c. *on* (not *in*) line, d. *train* (= subway), e. good *on* (not *for*) you

4. LaGuardia—LGA; Newark—EWR

5. Pink (Spalding's tennis ball minus the fuzz)

6. b.

7. At the uptown end of Times Square, between 45th and 47th Streets; it's the home of the TKTS booth, which dispenses reduced-price theater tickets (bonus: Francis P. Duffy was a priest and World War I military chaplain)

8. b. (bonus: a., e., and d. respectively)

9. a.-h., b.-f., c.-i., d.-g., e.-j.

10. "New York's Boldest"

11. a. Gray's Papaya; b. Papaya King

12. a. George Washington Bridge, b. Central Park West, c. Brooklyn Academy of Music, d. Museum of Modern Art, e. *Saturday Night Live*

13. Taxi and Limousine Commission

14. a. Queens, b. Brooklyn, c. Manhattan, d. Brooklyn, e. the Bronx

15. Queens (bonus: Forest Hills)

16. a. the *Post*, b. the *Daily News* (extra: the *Times*, of course)

17. Every year on the day before Thanksgiving, in preparation for Macy's Thanksgiving Day Parade

18. Queens Boulevard

19. BEAUTIFUL SKIN!

20. a.-j., b.-h., c.-f., d.-g., e.-i.

21. a.-h., b.-j., c.-f., d.-i., e.-g.

22. e.

23. a. Mayor Ed Koch, b. hotel and real estate figure Leona Helmsley

24. If you're Paul Simon and Art Garfunkel, you'd be doin' that in "The 59th Street Bridge Song (Feelin' Groovy)"

25. a. *Rosemary's Baby*, b. John Lennon, c. northwest, d. Strawberry Fields, e. at the time it was built, the area was so remote from the developed city that some suggested it might as well have been built in the Dakota Territory

26. a.-j., b.-i., c.-f., d.-g., e.-h.

27. c.

28. Wednesday

29. On Fifth Avenue, the Metropolitan Museum of Art; at Lincoln Center, the Metropolitan Opera

30. a. Unfinished, b. Woodlawn, c. better New York, d. tomato, e. Bronx Community College

31. a.-h., b.-f., c.-j., d.-i., e.-g.

32. "His prices are in-*sane!*"

33. c., b., f., e., a., g., d.

34. a. SOuth of Houston, b. TRiangle BElow CAnal, c. NOrth of Little ITAly, d. Down Under the Manhattan Bridge Overpass, e. area including Avenues A, B, C, and D

35. c.

36. Bennett Park

37. Videotape (or, on radio, audiotape)

38. e.

39. Casey Stengel, who played for the Dodgers (1912–17) and the Giants (1921–23), and managed the Dodgers (1934–36), the Yankees (1949–60), and the Mets (1962–65)

40. Shea—the #7 Flushing line; Aqueduct—the A train Rockaway line

41. Cheesecake

42. b.

43. a.-h., b.-j., c.-f., d.-i., e.-g.

44. "…How sweet it is!"

45. The world

46. a. Tiffany & Co., b. Bloomingdale's

47. a.-i., b.-j., c.-g., d.-h., e.-f.

48. g.

49. Eustace Tilley

50. a.

51. "Canyon of Heroes"

52. "*To your boy in the Army*" (bonus: the "I'll have what she's having" scene from *When Harry Met Sally*)

53. c.

54. Read the number on the small metal plate on the base of the nearest lamppost; the first two digits indicate the nearest cross street

55. Next number is 59 (street numbers of stops on the uptown West Side #1 subway line)

56. Stations d. and e. are news, b. and c. are news and talk, a. and f. are sports

57. She sang at Madison Square Garden, for a 45th birthday celebration for President John F. Kennedy ("Happy … birth … day … Mr. … Presi…dent…")

58. *The French Connection*

59. On Jeffrey's Hook, a smidgen of land extending into the Hudson River near a base of the George Washington Bridge; it inspired the children's book *The Little Red Lighthouse and the Great Gray Bridge*

60. The Flatiron Building

61. A Fox lock

62. Port Authority Trans Hudson

63. The Stonewall Inn on Christopher Street

64. a. and c.

65. Hotel Chelsea

66. Irv Gikofsky

67. a.-h. (building), b.-f. (airport), c.-j. (reservoir), d.-g. (building), e.-i. (neighborhood)

68. *Seinfeld* (bonus: Suzanne Vega, composer of "Tom's Diner")

69. "The Willy B" = The Williamsburg Bridge; "the George" = the George Washington Bridge

70. Carrie Bradshaw in the TV series *Sex and the City*

71. General

72. The Biltmore Garage

73. d.

74. *The Fantasticks*

75. a.-g., b.-j., c.-f., d.-h., e.-i.

76. Steve Brodie, who was said to have jumped off the Brooklyn Bridge and lived to brag about it, and whose name survived him in the expression "to pull a brodie"

77. "Take the A Train"

78. Earl Monroe (of the Knicks) and Joe Namath (of the Jets)

79. Washington Square Park

80. b.

81. Dr. Brown's

82. Van Cortlandt is about twice the size of Prospect

83. a. *Miracle on 34th Street*, b. *Crossing Delancey*, c. *Slaughter on Tenth Avenue*, d. *Broadway Danny Rose*, e. *The Panic in Needle Park*

84. a.–i., b.–h., c.–f., d.–j., e.–g.

85. It starts on Staten Island, near the approach to the Verrazano-Narrows Bridge; it finishes in Manhattan, at Tavern on the Green

86. The Strand (18 Miles of Books)

87. "An educated consumer is our best customer" (Syms clothing stores); "Please, Mr. D'Agostino, move closer to me" (D'Agostino's supermarkets)

88. c.

89. Donna Hanover

90. Mother Hale

91. a.–g., b.–j., c.–f., d.–h., e.–i.

92. Fay Wray is to the Empire State Building (the 1933 *King Kong* movie) as Jessica Lange is to the World Trade Center (the 1976 remake) as Naomi Watts is to the Empire State Building (the 2005 remake)

93. Kossar's is to bialys as Manganaro's is to hero sandwiches as John's on Bleecker is to pizza

94. School: "Little Red" (Little Red School House); ex-mayor: "Little Flower" (Fiorello LaGuardia)

95. Each park has a Wollman Rink for ice skating, open only in season

96. c.

97. Such a suggestion likely refers to the information booth above the clock in Grand Central's main concourse (bonus: four)

98. g.

99. A pair of lions (bonus: Patience and Fortitude)

100. e.